For Sohrab Godrej, friend, philanthropist and great soul.

This book has been inspired by **The India File,** a unit of programmes
in the **Eureka!** series, which was produced for Channel 4 Schools by YTV
and the International Broadcasting Trust.

Published by Channel Four Learning Limited and the IBT
with assistance from the Commission of the European Community.

Written by Zerbanoo Gifford, Director of the Asha Foundation

Illustrated by Jane Tattersfield and Holly Mann

Designed by Tim Shore, John Burke Design Consultancy

Edited by Adrienne Jones with Lynette Aitken

Celebrating India

परिचय
Introduction

Many people living in Britain have links with India through birth or family, and Indian culture is important in their daily lives: in dress, religion or language. For many others, school and the community, food, films and holidays may be their way of experiencing and understanding India. Whichever way we relate to India, we can all appreciate the varied way of life, the exciting culture and the important history of this vast nation.

India has an enormous variety of people and places. It is a country which is rich in both culture and industry. In the time of Queen Victoria, India was known as the 'jewel in the crown' of the British Empire and although India has been an independent, modern country, free from British rule since 1947, the bond between India and Britain is still strong.

One of the most beautiful sights in India, and probably the most famous building in the world, is the Taj Mahal. This building brings together much of the country's history and is recognised by many people as a symbol of India. Over 300 years after being built, it is still a wonderful sight. Made of white marble, its beauty is reflected in the still water of the gardens. It is here then, with the story of the Taj Mahal, that this book begins.

The Taj Mahal

The Taj Mahal was built in the city of Agra, next to the Jumna river, in the north of India. Shah Jahan, a powerful Mogul emperor who ruled much of India, ordered the work on the Taj Mahal to begin in 1631. It was to be a tomb in memory of his wife Mumtaz and took nearly 20 years to finish.

The name Taj Mahal comes from Mumtaz's nickname, 'crown of the palace'. Shah Jahan was a Muslim and in Islam, religious buildings are not allowed to contain pictures of people. Instead, the inside walls are decorated with beautiful patterns made with semi-precious stones.

The Taj Mahal has many stories attached to it. The best known of these tells of the two loves of Shah Jahan. The first was his wife, Mumtaz, and the second was his rose garden.

Mumtaz had many children. During one of her pregnancies, she complained to Shah Jahan about feeling uncomfortable. He told her off for complaining and reminded her that most women in his kingdom gave birth in the fields without help from doctors and servants. Perhaps, he asked, she would like to do without help too?

Mumtaz was upset at this and wanted to make her husband understand. So she ordered the head gardener to stop watering, pruning and weeding the emperor's favourite roses. As the weeks passed, the roses began to die. When Shah Jahan asked Mumtaz for advice, she told him that in his kingdom most roses grew happily in the wild, without any help from gardeners, so she had told the gardeners to stop looking after them. Shah Jahan was furious, but he realised that his wife had taught him an important lesson: for anything or anybody to do well and be happy, you have to give them care and attention.

It took over 20,000 workers to build the Taj Mahal. It is said that the hands of many of the builders were cut off on the orders of Shah Jahan, because he wanted to make sure that they could never build anything like it again. Such cruelty was one of the reasons why Shah Jahan was overthrown by his son, who put him in a prison across the river from the Taj Mahal. Although he could never again visit the magnificent tomb he had built for his wife, it is said that he looked at it every day and wept.

ইতিহাস
History

Like Britain, India has seen many different groups of people arrive, settle and become part of the country. Some have come as conquerors, some as traders and some as refugees.

 India gets her name from the Indus people, who lived in the valley of the Indus river. Five thousand years ago, when people in Britain lived in wood and mud huts, many Indus people lived in towns with two- and three-storey houses. Their houses often had a separate room for washing. These were the world's first bathrooms! However, for some unknown reason, the Indus people abandoned their cities about 3,500 years ago.

Later, the Aryan people from Persia (Iran) began a new civilisation along India's other great river, the Ganges. There followed a time of many kingdoms in India.

Empires

 India's first great empire, or kingdom, was founded around 327 BC, when King Chandragupta ruled most of north-west and central India. After his reign several invasions from the north caused changes throughout India.

Muslims came as traders sailing from Arabia and visited the ports along the west coast. They were impressed with Indian mathematics and astronomy. Some settled peacefully but others invaded the north of India and formed an empire there. Most rulers of the empire were Muslims, but their subjects were mostly Hindus.

Barbur founded the Mogul Empire in 1526. Its greatest ruler, Akbar, tried to bring together Islamic and Hindu culture. Akbar died in 1605, soon after the start of the British trading company that eventually took over India.

The Indus People

The Aryans

King Chandragupta

Barbu

3000 BC   1500 BC   327 BC   1526

The East India Company was given permission by England's Queen Elizabeth I to trade with India. They bought land, built forts and formed their own army to protect their trade in spices and cotton. Gradually, more and more of India came under the East India Company's control. Some local rulers sold their kingdoms but in other cases land was deliberately invaded. Some Indian kings were strongly against British control. One of them, Tipu Sultan, nicknamed the Tiger of Mysore, even had a moving model made of a tiger eating an East India Company soldier.

By 1850, the East India Company ruled more people in India than the entire population of Britain. Seven years later, the Indian soldiers in the company's army rebelled against the British. Many people were killed. Control of India was taken away from the East India Company. India then became part of Britain's world-wide empire ruled by Queen Victoria. She was said to be delighted at having this new country in the British Empire and learnt some Hindi.

Emperor Akbar

East India Company Official

East India Company soldier

Queen Victoria

1556–1605   1760   1857   1868

ગાંધી Gandhi

Mohandas Gandhi was born in India in 1869. He did well at school and at the age of 13 he married Kasturbai, in the traditional Hindu custom of child marriages. Gandhi went to London to study law in September 1888, leaving Kasturbai and his first son. He became a lawyer in June 1891 and sailed for home. Gandhi believed in Satyagraha – the force of truth and love. When faced with a law he thought was unfair, he would protest peacefully by breaking the law and accepting the punishment. He encouraged everyone to do the same.

 One famous campaign was about salt. All salt had to be bought from the British who added on extra tax when they sold it to the people of India. As a protest, the 61-year-old Gandhi walked 241 miles to the sea to collect salt. Hundreds of people walked with him. This was a powerful but peaceful demonstration against British rule. More than 10,000 people were imprisoned and everybody stopped working.

 In 1919, British troops in Amritsar were ordered to kill hundreds of unarmed demonstrators. This massacre made people want independence for India.

Gandhi was asked to come to London to discuss independence. The *dhoti* that he wore became famous throughout Britain. Sometimes he would be greeted by children shouting, 'Gandhi, where's your

1869   1872   1888   1891   1892   1915

Gandhi outside number 10 Downing Street

By the end of the Second World War in 1945, India was almost impossible to rule. There was widespread violence. The end of British rule was arranged as quickly as possible. India was divided into two separate countries – India with mostly Hindus and Pakistan with mostly Muslims. This was called 'Partition'. Many people were unhappy at the idea of Partition. There was more violence and many people were killed. Gandhi himself was shot dead by a Hindu who mistakenly thought that he supported Partition. Sadly, he had not  listened to Gandhi's teaching that you do not need to use violence to change things.

trousers?' Gandhi was introduced to King George V. Asked afterwards if he should have worn more clothes, Gandhi replied, 'The King was wearing enough for two people.'

The first Indian Prime Minister, who was called Jawaharlal Nehru, had a very important part in Indian independence. He also made one of the century's most famous speeches, on the 14th August 1947, when he said, 'at the stroke of the midnight hour, when the world sleeps, India will awake to life and freedom'.

1919   1930   1931   1947   1948

Religion

Brahma and Saraswati, Vishnu and Lakshmi, Shiva and Parvati

Several of the world's great religions have their origins in India, particularly Hinduism, Buddhism, Sikhism and Jainism. Many other world religions have also found a home there, for example India has more Christians than Britain.

Hinduism

Around eight out of ten Indians are Hindus. Hinduism has developed over the past 4,000 years. It is one of the world's oldest faiths. Much of Hindu belief was not originally written down, but was passed on through story telling. The stories changed slightly through time and this has led to many different strands of Hinduism.

Hindus believe that there are many gods and goddesses. The three major gods are *Brahma* the creator, *Vishnu* the protector and *Shiva* who both destroys and generates new life. These gods, like everyone, are filled with a supreme spirit, *Brahman*.

Hindus also believe that when people die, their souls will live on to be reborn into another body. This new form may be better or worse than before – it depends on how the person has behaved. Hindus pray for help to be good, so that they become something better in their next life.

As part of their daily worship, known as *puja*, many Hindus will worship at home or visit a temple. Most homes have a small household shrine to a particular god. Each day, offerings of food, flowers or incense will be made, along with readings from scriptures.

Islam

Islam is an Arabic word meaning 'surrender to Allah'. Its followers are known as Muslims. The *Qur'an* is Islam's holy book. It sets out five 'rules' of Islamic life for Muslims to follow. The first and most important duty of a Muslim is to recognise that there is only one God, Allah, and that Muhammad is His Messenger. The second is *salat*, prayer, carried out five times a day while facing Mecca, the Holy city. The third is *zakat*, giving money to charity each year. The fourth is *sawm*, a fast during the hours of daylight for the Islamic month of Ramadan. The fifth, *haji*, is a pilgrimage to Mecca.

Christianity

Christianity arrived in India from different countries. Wherever Europeans settled, there were missionaries who came to convert some of the local population to Christianity.

Jainism

Jainism dates from around 550 BC. Jains believe that all life is sacred, and that the taking of life is a very serious sin. Jain monks often wear masks over their mouths to stop them accidentally killing insects by breathing them into their mouths. Most followers are not this strict, but they are vegetarian and try not to eat animal products like honey.

Statue of the Buddha

Buddhism

Buddhism was founded in India by Siddhartha Gautama, around 540 BC. The Buddha, or 'enlightened one', as he became known, was the son of a wealthy local ruler in the southern Himalayas. It is said that when riding around his city of Kapilavastu in a chariot, he saw much suffering. The Buddha said that people's suffering was caused by greed. In order to help people be free from suffering, he created the 'Eightfold Path', which is based on being wise, kind, fair and disciplined.

Zoroastrianism

Zoroastrianism was founded in Persia (now Iran) around 3,500 years ago by a man called Zoroaster. Zoroastrians worship one God called Ahura Mazda. They believe that people must try to work for good, to make the world a better place. It is the duty of all human beings to have good thoughts, use good words and do good deeds. After death, it is believed that the actions of each person will be judged.

The story of what happened in a small fishing village in Gujarat is a very special one for Zoroastrians. The Zoroastrian

rcfugees were taken in front of the local Hindu ruler. He explained that his country was too crowded and there was no room for new settlers. To show this, he took a bowl and filled it with water until it was so full that not one more drop could be added. But the Zoroastrian High Priest called for a little sugar. He carefully put it into the bowl. It dissolved without spilling any of the water. 'Perhaps your land is full, but we will sweeten it with our presence, without changing any of your people or your customs,' he said.

The Zoroastrians became known as Parsis – people from Persia.

Sikhism

Guru Nanak was the founder of Sikhism. He wanted to join together Hinduism and Islam and ended up making a new religion separate from both of these. Another famous Guru or leader, called Ram Das, started building the city of Amritsar. It is now the home of the Golden Temple, which is the Sikhs' holiest place of worship. Long ago, Sikhs also created the *Khalsa*, an army to defend against prejudice. Its members wore the five 'K's: *kesh* (uncut hair and beard), *kangha* (comb), *kirpan* (sword), *kara* (steel bracelet) and *kachera* (short trousers). The men also wore a turban. Some of the five 'K's can be seen in the followers of Sikhism today.

A follower of Sikhism

भारत
India

From the high Himalayan mountains in the north to the Nilgiri hills in the south, India is a huge country full of great contrasts.

In Rajasthan, next to the border with Pakistan, lies the Thar desert. It hardly rains at all here. By contrast, eastern India, near Bangladesh, may have more than 1,080 centimetres of rain a year. Living in the north near Tibet can be cold and the rocky soil means that not much food can be grown. However, in the south of India the climate is warm and the soil very fertile.

ਰੇਲਵੇਜ਼

The Railways

When the British ruled India, they built the railways. Bombay, Madras and Calcutta were the first three ports of British India. They were all on the coast and could be reached by ship, but the weather often made this difficult. Also, as the British moved further inland, traditional methods of travel, such as horseback riding (for rich people), or carts or walking (for the poor), meant that journeys took weeks or even months.

The building of railways by the British solved this. After much hard work by Indian labourers, a network of railways was built between India's major cities. Trade increased, with trains carrying huge loads of goods long distances to the ports where they were taken to Europe and sold. It also meant that newspapers could be published nationally, and not be too out of date when they arrived on the other side of the country.

The great city stations were often built to remind the British of home. Bombay has a Victoria Station just like the one in London. The main station in the holy city of Varanasi, on the other hand, was designed to look like a Hindu temple.

Railways were one of the great wonders of the Victorian age. One Indian prince even built a toy railway to serve guests at his dining table. Trains ran around on top of the table carrying the food to each person.

Much of India is perfect for railways as it is flat or slopes very gently. However, in India's mountainous areas smaller trains run on tracks known as narrow-gauge railways. Some of India's best-loved routes use narrow-gauge trains to climb up to the 'hill stations' of Darjeeling and Simla, where the British rulers of India used to spend the summers away from the heat. Railways are for many the favourite way of travelling around India.

The rail network is the fourth largest in the world, with over 60,000 kilometres of track – enough to go around the world one and a half times! Around 11 million people use India's railways every day. Some trains are so crowded that people even sit on the luggage racks!

For the many people in villages with no station nearby, most long journeys are made by bus. Only about two in every thousand people own a car, and most cars are in cities. To travel around their local area, people use bicycles, auto-rickshaws (motorised, three-wheel bicycle taxis) or walk.

বৃটেন থেকে ভারত
From Britain to India

over one year

Travelling between India and Britain has become much easier than it once was. Until a few hundred years ago, the journey would have taken over a year. The discovery of the sea route around Africa in the 15th century meant the journey could be done by one ship in just a few months. The next big cut in travelling time was when the Suez Canal was built in 1869. This shortened the journey time to about a month.

a few months

With the invention of aeroplanes at the start of this century, the journey time tumbled again. The first passenger flights between the two countries started in the 1930s and it became possible to travel to India in a few days. Today, travel by jet aircraft means you can leave Britain and be in India in just under nine hours.

one month

a few days

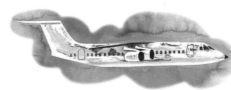

under nine hours

BRITAIN

INDIA

જંગલી પશુપંખી
Wildlife

The national bird of India is the peacock. It is found all over India and in some places is quite tame. However, India is also known as 'the land of the tiger'. Perhaps the most famous Indian tiger is Sher Khan, 'Tiger King', in *The Jungle Book* by Rudyard Kipling. Kipling lived in India for many years and learned to speak Hindi. This is why he called most of the characters in his story by their Hindi names. *Sher* means tiger, *Bhalu* is Hindi for bear, *Bandar* is monkey, *Hathi* means elephant. The book showed the many different varieties of animals in India and has been made into a well-known Disney film.

In the days when *The Jungle Book* was written, there were about 40,000 tigers living in India's forests. Sadly, the number of tigers is a lot smaller today. There are many reasons for this. Hunters thought that killing a tiger was a great achievement and many came to India just to win a trophy. Tiger skin coats used to be fashionable. It took six dead tigers to make one coat. Some tigers were poisoned by villagers who blamed them for eating farm animals, while many more died because the forest homes of the tiger were cut down to create more land to farm.

By 1972 the number of Indian tigers had fallen to just 2,000. The World Wildlife Fund for Nature launched an international appeal for help. In response, the Indian government set up 'Project Tiger' and India now has 23 tiger reserves where these magnificent animals live in safety, and tiger hunting is banned.

However, tigers are really clever at hiding in their dense forest homes, so it can be very difficult to count them. So to estimate the number of tigers in an area, people count pugmarks (tiger footprints) instead. According to these estimates, India now has around 3,000 tigers. Unfortunately, poaching and illegal hunting still continue. Poachers kill tigers for money because some people believe that the skin and bones can be used as medicine.

Protecting the rest of the natural environment is also important to India which has more than 100 wildlife sanctuaries and national parks.

மொழிகளும்
Language

One effect of India's large size and long history is that there are 18 official languages. The most common Indian language is Hindi, which is spoken as the main language by about one fifth of the population. Other important languages include Urdu, Bengali, Gujarati, Kashmiri, Sindhi and Marathi.

One of the oldest languages is Sanskrit, still in use today. It was used for many of the sacred texts of Hindus, Buddhists and Jains. The first book on the rules and grammar of any language was written by an Indian scholar called Panini. He was the first person to write down 4,000 rules of Sanskrit around 400 BC.

English   My homework usually takes me about half an hour.

Hindi   मुझे घर की पढ़ाई के काम में अधिकतर करीब आधे घंटे लगते है

Bengali   আমার হোমওয়ার্ক করতে আধ ঘন্টার মত লাগে ।

Gujarati   મારું હોમવર્ક કરતાં મને સાધારણ અડધો કલાક લાગે.

Panjabi   ਮੇਰਾ ਹੋਮ ਵਰਕ ਅੱਧੇ ਘੰਟੇ ਵਿਚ ਪੂਰਾ ਹੋ ਜਾਂਦਾ ਹੈ ।

Tamil   எனது வீட்டு வேலை வழமையாக அரை மணி நேரம் எடுக்கும்.

Urdu   میرا اسکول کا کام عموماً آدھے گھنٹے میں ختم ہو جاتا ہے ۔

अं
अ इ उ
अ इ ऋ ऌ उ

क च ट त प
ख छ ठ थ फ
ग ज ड द ब
घ झ ढ ध म
ङ ञ ण न स

ह य र ल व
श ष स
अं
अः

The Sanskrit alphabet

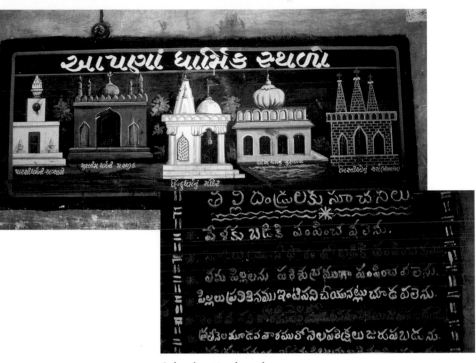

School notice boards

In 1786, Sir William Jones, a British man serving in India, realised that Indian languages were related to English. He said that Sanskrit was a 'wonderful language, and the root of all other languages, more perfect than Greek and richer than Latin.' Experts in language now call this ancient language 'Indo-European'. Much is known about it even though it was only spoken by a small group of people about 6,000 years ago. We can even guess what it sounded like.

Some of the rules of the Indo-European languages can still be seen in English today. For example, we say more than one foot are 'feet' rather than 'foots' and more than one tooth are 'teeth' rather than 'tooths'. This language spread to different areas, changing along the way. It is the root of the wide variety of languages spoken in India and Europe today.

One result of British rule in India is that English is one of India's official languages. It is often spoken when people who speak different Indian languages want to communicate with each other. Many of the country's newspapers and magazines are also in English.

The English language helps to bring the two countries closer and to allow the people of India and Britain to learn from each other. English has been made richer by lots of words from India.

Thanks to these words, English speakers can describe:

a 'cushy' life in a 'bungalow' while drinking 'punch'

and eating 'curry'. They can wear a 'chintz' 'shawl'

when changing a baby's 'dungarees' and putting on her 'pyjamas'

before putting her in a 'cot'. But with luck, they will never have 'thugs'

'loot' their home, or be lost in a 'jungle'.

Certain other Indian words are now well-known in Britain too, but are not yet part of the English language. Many relate to food, like *poppadum*, *vindaloo*, or *naan*. Perhaps they will soon become as much a part of the English language as potato or pizza.

ਗਣਿਤ
Maths

India has a long history of mathematics. Books written about astronomy in about AD 500 even show numbers and fractions. About AD 800, a set of numerals known as the *Devanagri* numerals appeared. These were different from all other numbers before them because they were based on place value. Our numbers today are almost the same. These Hindu numbers were what are called single code symbols, unlike Roman numerals, when an '8' has to be written as 'VIII' or '9' as 'IX'. Single code numbers were even more important when it came to writing them down.

	1	2	3	4	5	6	7	8	9	10
Bengali	১	২	৩	৪	৫	৬	৭	৮	৯	১০
Hindu	?	?	?	?	?	?	?	?	?	?
Urdu	١	٢	٣	٤	٥	٦	٧	٨	٩	١٠

Hindu merchants who bought and sold goods needed an extra number to add to the nine they already had, so invented the zero. At first zero stood for an empty space. For example, how could we write a large number like 5,070 without a zero? It might be written as 5,7, but then it could be mistaken for 57. When the zero, or *sunya* as the Hindus called it, became an actual number, sums could then be added and multiplied more easily.

One of the most important discoveries in the history of mathematics is the number zero. It is the zero which makes our numbers easy to handle.

Rangoli patterns

Maths and art are closely linked in India. Rangoli, or Alpana as it is known in some areas of India, is a form of folk art used to decorate the floors of homes and shrines with patterns of coloured chalk. Originally rice was used.

Rangoli floor patterns are based on a shape. The shape, which is a square, a rectangle or a circle, is made using pinches of coloured powder or dots of coloured chalk. The pattern, which is usually symmetrical, is then added.

Rangoli are usually done by the women, who often sing songs about the pattern as they work. The patterns, which are traditional, may be a symmetrical geometric pattern, or include a picture of a flower, fruit, tree or person. Rangoli can also be adapted for patchwork, printmaking or cross-stitch embroidery.

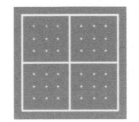

Step 1

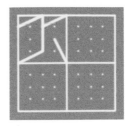

Step 2

Step 3

Step 4

Step 5

জ্যোতিষ-শাস্ত্র
Astrology

Astrology is an ancient Indian mathematical science. Only the high priests were allowed to practise this science.

In the past, many Indians consulted an astrologer before starting something new and they still do today.

The astrologer works out the positions of the stars and planets and will then try to predict whether the signs are good. If the astrologer thinks the signs are not good, the start of the project is often put off until a more favourable date.

Astrologers are often asked to predict the success or failure of partnerships, including marriages, by looking at the charts for the people involved. Many families will ask an astrologer to draw up a birth chart for each new-born child so they can help plan for the future. In some cases they may even choose the baby's name according to the astrologer's suggestions.

In Indian astrology the sky is divided into 12 areas, or signs, based on particular patterns of the stars. By working out the position of the sun, the moon and the planets in the 12 signs at the time and date of someone's birth, a pattern can be drawn on a chart. The astrologer then looks for particular features, such as the sign on the horizon. This is said to give an idea of a person's character.

Today, many astrologers in India's cities use computers to help their work. Once the astrologers are given the exact time and place of birth, they can provide their clients with many pages of individual predictions. These often include suggestions as to which dates in the future are especially favourable and on which days the astrologer believes they should be particularly careful.

Games

Many of the games played around the world today were invented in India. The children's game snakes and ladders was originally called *Moksha-patamu*. This was used to teach children about the importance of good behaviour. Good deeds, represented by the ladders, made the journey towards wisdom shorter, but bad deeds meant slipping back and being born again as an animal, such as a snake, in the next life.

Chess comes from the game *Shaturanga*, which was played in India over 1,500 years ago. Two teams of two players, each with an army of eight pieces, took turns in throwing dice to decide which piece they could move. At the start, players and spectators often placed bets on which side would win. When gambling was made illegal in India, people caught playing *Shaturanga* were punished so the rules of the game were changed and the dice removed.

The next major change was to make it a game for two players, by combining each team's armies into one of sixteen pieces. If you have ever wondered why each side in modern chess has two bishops, two knights and two rooks, it is because they were originally in two separate armies. The game then spread to the rest of the world through Persia.

Another Indian game, *Pachisi*, is an ancestor of ludo. Players move their pieces by throwing cowrie shells rather than dice, and each player has to start and finish in the same square. Several Indian rulers built *Pachisi* boards on the

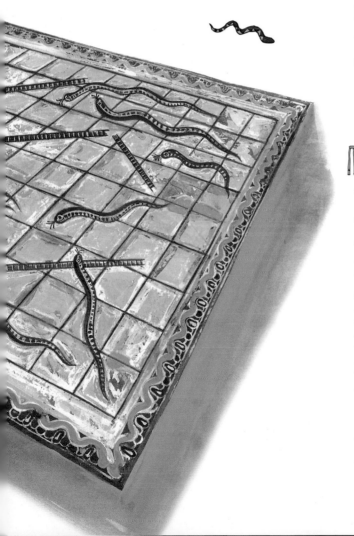

floors of their palaces and used their servants as pieces!

Snooker was also invented in India. In 1875, a British army officer, Neville Chamberlain, combined the rules of two games – billiards and pyramids – to create snooker.

Outdoors, both hockey and cricket are very popular in India. India's hockey team has long been one of the best in the world. It won Gold medals at the Olympic Games six times in a row.

Cricket was one of the first things brought to India by the British. The Calcutta Cricket Club was started in 1792, not long after the start of the MCC, the Marylebone Cricket Club, in England. The first Indian team to tour Britain, the Parsi Cricket Club of Bombay, arrived in 1886, just four years after the first test matches between England and Australia. Before Indian Independence, several Indian players were members of the England team, including two Indian princes. Today, India remains one of the leading cricketing nations and test matches played in India attract thousands of passionate fans.

કામ

Work

Before Independence in 1947, much of India's industry was owned or run by the British. When the new Indian government took over, one of the first things they wanted to do was to produce everything that people need within India itself. Today Indian industry makes everything from computers and cars to cloth and chemicals, from steel and sugar cane to scooters and ships.

Around 5,000 years ago, the Indus people were the first to wear cotton clothes. Since then, India has remained a major producer of cotton. Although India was the world's largest producer of cotton, it had no large mills of its own. Instead, the British rulers paid a small amount for Indian cotton, and then shipped it to mills in Britain. Many of the clothes were then sold back to India at a high price. This kind of business still happens today and is one reason why much of the wealth of many poorer countries ends up in the hands of richer countries.

Those Indians who could not afford to buy the clothes made in Britain, made their own by hand. Mahatma Gandhi's dream of a self-sufficient India was based on weaving cotton as small village businesses, but Indian leaders wanted larger, more efficient, modern businesses. One mill in Bombay is the largest textile factory in Asia. Today India is a highly industrialised country. Many companies have gone to India because of its natural resources, its modern technology and low wages. Children who work are paid the lowest wages of all.

Industry can also create health and safety problems. Fumes from cars pollute cities, while other industries do damage by polluting the local rivers.

Although most of India's industries are based in her cities, about three-quarters of the population live in the countryside. India has about 650,000 villages of about 1,000 people each. Just over half of the people in India work in farming or fishing. There are 25 million people involved in rice growing alone.

फ़िल्म उद्योग
The Film Industry

One of the most famous – and largest – industries in India today, is the film industry. It is the second largest in the world (the USA have the largest) and makes nearly 1,000 films each year. Bombay is the centre of India's film world and is nicknamed 'Bollywood', after Hollywood in the United States.

Most Indian films are musicals. Songs are obviously important in musicals, but they are very hard to film live. The noise of the equipment and the high cost of mistakes means that film makers have to record the song in a recording studio first. This recording is then played back in the film studio and the actors mime the words. In western musicals, the actor in the film is nearly always the same person who sings the song. Only if the actor has a poor singing voice is another person asked to sing and the actor mimes. However, in Indian films, the same 'playback' singers are always used – it doesn't matter who the actors are. The most famous 'playback' singer is Lata Mangeshkar, who is in *The Guinness Book of Records* for having sung more songs than anyone else in the world.

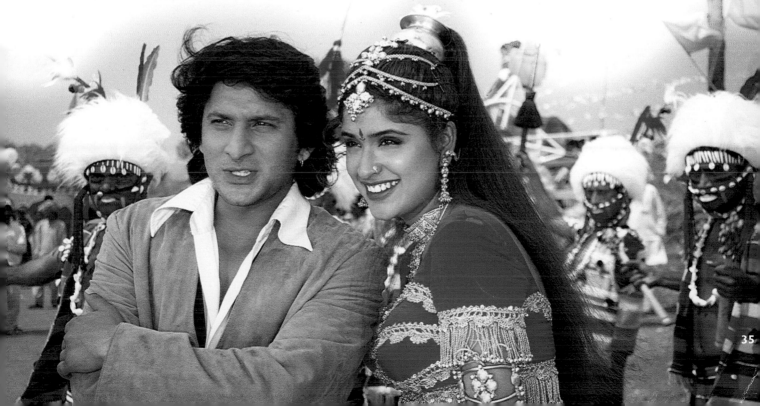

உடுபுகளும்
Clothes

India is one of the few countries where you see people wearing their national costume every day. Most women across India wear a sari. This is a six-metre length of material which is wrapped around the waist to make a skirt, draped over the front of a blouse (*choli*) and then hung over the shoulder. The end of the material is left hanging or put around the head, depending on the occasion. Saris range from simple colours in cotton to complicated designs traced on expensive fabrics, like silk, with borders of gold or silver threads.

Many other women also wear a printed cotton sari, with a chiffon scarf, white baggy trousers (*shalwar*), and sandals. Young women like to combine traditional dress and today's fashion. They wear trousers and a long shirt called a *khameez*.

Men's clothing varies more from region to region, but in cities across India, many men wear suits. Other men wear the traditional *kurta*, which is a collarless shirt, with a *dhoti*, which was

made famous by Mahatma Gandhi. A *dhoti* is a long piece of thin material which is tied around the waist. The loose end is drawn up between the legs and tucked in at the waist. This makes a loose pair of trousers which are cool and practical for the climate of India. In cooler weather a woollen waistcoat is worn over the *kurta*.

Certain clothes have a religious function, like the turban Sikh men are expected to wear over their uncut hair. Other famous Indian clothes include jodhpurs, named after the riding trousers worn by the Maharaja of Jodhpur. Many other clothes worn throughout the world are made from Indian cotton.

Some items of clothing are named after the famous people who wore them. People today still wear Wellington boots, named after the Duke of Wellington, who served in India as a soldier and a governor.

Similarly, men's collarless jackets are known around the world as Nehru jackets, after the first Indian Prime Minister, Jawaharlal Nehru.

37

Naan

A type of roti, made using yoghurt

Chappati

A type of roti, made from atta flour and water

Puri

A round, savoury snack mad...

Food

Food was one of the main reasons why Europeans first sailed to India 500 years ago. Early traders were looking for the spices that fetched high prices in Britain. This link between the two countries continues today. Nearly every British high street has an Indian restaurant or take-away, while supermarkets now sell ranges of Indian food to cook at home.

In India, the favourite food varies from region to region. Some of these differences are due to religious beliefs, for example the *Qur'an* forbids Muslims to eat pork. All Hindus are forbidden beef, because the cow is regarded as a sacred animal. Some Hindus, like Jains and many people in Gujarat, are vegetarian. Most Gujarati food is made from vegetables, beans and pulses.

People from Goa eat a lot of fish. This is due to the influence of the Portuguese who once ruled Goa. Bengali cooking also often uses fish, which can be very spicy because of the chilli peppers in it.

South Indian food is often flavoured with coconut or fruits like lemons or limes, while Punjabi food is based around lamb and chicken. In some areas, cooks use a clay tandoori oven, while in others plenty of cooking pans are used.

Pakora

Deep-fried vegetable savouries

A type of roti, made from atta flour, water and ghee

Paratha

Sambhar

Roti

hole-wheat flour and deep fried

Lightly cooked cabbage, carrots, chillies and tumeric

Flat bread made without yeast

Side dish of plain yoghurt with cucumber

Raita

Rice, spices and milk are found in nearly all regions. Rice is one of the world's major food crops, and is grown wherever there is plenty of water. Spices preserve food in hot climates, and also add flavour to a meal. Milk is often used in the form of yoghurt or *ghee* (a type of butter) which helps to preserve it.

Most Indian people love to eat snacks during the day. Fast-food shops and roadside cafes and stalls offer everything from curried meat and vegetables in batter to chickpeas, yoghurt and lentil dishes. These are often served in leaves or wrapped into a samosa, ready to take away. Leaves are used, instead of plastic or paper, as it is both cheaper and better for the environment. Special meals are often served in large banana leaves or on little dishes on a large metal plate. Street sellers also sell a delicious range of fresh fruit juices.

When a train arrives at a station in India, food sellers jump on board, or walk alongside the train, trying to sell their snacks. As well as savoury foods, there are many delicious Indian sweets, which are very rich and often contain plenty of milk, *ghee*, pistachios, almonds and cashew nuts.

Melted butter

Ghee

filled pasties

A pudding made with dried milk, boiled until thick

Thin crispy bread wafers

Samosa

Halwa

Poppadums

নৃত্য
Dance

Indian dance is a way of expressing beauty and harmony in movement. There are different styles of dance all over India from classical to folk.

Some of the classical dances are like ballet and are over 1,000 years old. Dance movement is shown in some of the ancient sculptures. In classical dance the expression in the eyes, and the movements of the hands and feet have a special meaning. Often the dance is based on a hymn, a poem in praise of God or a story. The movement is full of grace and rhythm. Sometimes there is music and singing to accompany the movement.

Here are some hand movements from classical dance:

Tripataka (fire)   **Mayura (peacock)**   **Hamsasya (swan)**

Both men and women can take part in folk dancing. There are numerous variations in the dances depending on the region. A group of dancers may work out their own sets of movements, and dancers and musicians work together to create the dance.

Here are two dances from the Gujarat area:

Dandya ras

This is danced by men only, women only, or both together. It is danced either in a circle or in lines with two rows of people facing each other. Any number of dancers may be involved. It is danced using a wooden stick called a *dandya* stick, about 30 centimetres long and two centimetres in diameter. Often, especially in regions like Gujarat, the stick is beautifully painted, with a tassel at the end. When a *dandya ras* is danced in a circle, two sticks are used, but when it is danced in a line, one stick is enough.

Ras gharba

This is usually danced in a circle by women only. Clapping provides the rhythm, but often the lead dancers may wear a *janjer*, an ankle bracelet with small bells that jangles when the women walk. This also helps the dancers to stay in rhythm. The women would usually accompany themselves by singing *gharba* songs, but sometimes a group of musicians on *tabla* or harmonium accompany the dancers.

Music

موسیقی

Sangeet is the Hindi word for music. Music has always been important in India and there are many varieties of musical instruments.

As in dance, there is classical and folk music. Classical music is performed by a small group of musicians made up of the main artist who is a singer or *sitar* player, accompanied by players on the flute, the *tamboura* (a simple instrument with four strings) and a pair of *tabla* drums.

Many of the tunes are made up as the musicians play. The music is often fast and exciting, the rhythm is strong and the tunes rise and fall in a scale. Indian music is based on *ragas*, which are special tunes.

Tabla
A kind of drum in two parts, each with a skin stretched across the top. Used in northern India for both classical and film music.

Damru
A small drum that can be carried about in one hand. Used to accompany folk dances.

There are special *ragas* for morning to help you wake up, and for early evening to calm and soothe you.

Film and pop music is based on classical traditions but also uses folk and religious tunes and rhythms. One type of Indian music you might have heard in this country is *bhangra*.

Bhangra was originally from the Punjab and is now very popular in Britain. Equally, *bhangra* produced in Britain is well liked in India.

There are many percussion instruments used in Indian music. Some are very simple and are made from pots and pans, others are very complex and are difficult to play.

Khundjri
A small open framed drum, beaten with the hands, similar to a tambourine.

Veena and Sitar
Classical stringed instruments with long necks and metal strings.

Pakhwaj
Made of wood, sometimes with bells or brass discs attached. Both pieces are held in the same hand and used like castanets.